Clatteringshaws Loch

THE SOUTHERN UPLAND WAY, ST. CUTHBERT'S WAY, LANARKSHIRE BASTLES TRAIL, AND THE JOHN MUIR WAY

Mike Salter

FOLLY PUBLICATIONS

Lindisfarne Priory

ACKNOWLEDGEMENTS

Sylvia Campbell took the back cover photograph and the view of the Three Brethren on page 25, and also helped with transport. Charles Henderson took the picture of Thirlestane Castle on page 28. Kate Miles contributed the picture of Lauder Church on page 29. The other photographs are from Mike Salter's collections, and he also drew the maps. He walked the Portpatrrick to Melrose part of the Southern Upland Way and the Bastles Trail in eight days during June 2005, and the Melrose to Cockburnspath part of the trail was walked over two days in September 2005. Mike walked the Hawick to Melrose part of the Borders Abeys Way and the St Cuthbert's Way over six days in September 2006, and the John Muir Trail between Cockburnspath and East Linton was walked in January 2007. Thanks to the staff at Aspect Design for their help in preparing illustrations and generally assembling the artwork of the book ready for publication.

DISCLAIMER

Every effort has been made to ensure information in this book is accurate and up-to-date, but the author/publisher does not accept any responsibility for any accidents to users, nor is any responsibility accepted for any problems that might arise through any of the information given being inaccurate, incomplete or out-of-date. Please take careful note of the suggestions about outdoor safety given on page 8.

AUTHOR'S NOTES

Distances are given in miles, still the most familiar unit of measurement for most British people. Although modern Ordnance Survey maps are metric, heights and amounts of climb in this book are given in feet, mainly so as to avoid any ambiguity as to whether an m folowing a figure means miles or metres. The contours on the Landranger maps are at 10 metre intervals, i.e. crossing three of them means roughly 100 feet of climb.

ABOUT THE AUTHOR

Mike Salter is 53 and has been a professional author and publisher since 1988. He is particularly interested in the planning and layout of medieval buildings and has a huge collection of plans of castles and old churches he has measured during tours (mostly by bicycle and motorcycle) throughout all parts of the British Isles since 1968. Wolverhampton born and bred, Mike now lives in an old cottage beside the Malvern Hills. Since walking Land's End to John O'Groats in 2004 following his 50th birthday he has done many other long distance backpacking trails. He is a life member of both the YHA and English Heritage, and he is also a member of the Backpackers Club and the Mountain Bothies Association. His other interests include railways, board games, morris dancing and calling folk dances and playing percussion with an occasional ceilidh band.

Melrose Abbey

CONTENTS

INDRODUCTION

THE SOUTHERN UPLAND WAY

Originally created in 1984, and provided with minor new diversions and some new signs in 2004-5, the Southern Upland Way is the longest and toughest route-marked walking trail in Scotland. At 212 miles long it is more than twice the length of the West Highland Way, and it requires greater navigational skills because of extensive forest and moorland sections with only a bare minimum of guide-posts marked with a thistle set in a hexagon. Some of the moorland sections have little in the way of actual path to follow. Although the Southern Uplands are lower and softer in outline than the mountains of the Highlands, the walking is every bit as tough. The paths are less frequented and the supply points are further apart and generally less geared to tourists. With a 26 mile gap between St John's Town of Dalry and Sanquhar, the Southern Upland Way is the least well provided for in terms of bed and breakfast accommodation of all Britain's route-marked trails. Not many people walk the complete route in one go and most will carry sleeping bags and mats for use in the six bothies which lie on or near the route, if not tents as well. To attempt even part of this route you'll need to be fit, well-shod, experienced in hill-walking and able to carry a fair amount of weight in a pack. Access to the Way is mostly by buses since drastic pruning of the railways and stations in the Scottish Lowlands has left only Sanquhar with a station close to the route (see page 9).

This book assumes that you'll walk the way from west to east since this is by far the best direction to go, with the prevailing wind and afternoon sun tending to be behind you. May is a good time for the walk, with long days, midges not yet a serious problem, probably dry weather, and no worries about disturbing either lambing ewes found earlier in the season or the shooting parties which may be out later in the year. Very few people will complete the walk in under ten days and most should allow a fortnight or so.

THE ST CUTHBERT'S WAY AND THE JOHN MUIR WAY

Although easier than the Southern Upland Way, the 64 mile route of the St Cuthbert's Way is still quite demanding and will take most people four or five days to complete. Note that the tidal causeway to Holy Island is not safe to cross for more than half of a tidal cycle and this may delay you by several hours. This book assumes that you will be starting at Melrose and heading east to Holy Island as this makes a wonderful finish.

As the Melrose to Cockburnspath section of the Souithern Upland Way is somewhat easier to walk and navigate than the sections of extensive forest and bare moorland further west, some walkers may like to consider possibilities such as combining this eastern section of the Southern Upland Way with St Cuthbert's Way for a 109 mile trail from Cockburnspath to Holy Island via Melrose, which should be achievable in seven or eight days. Faster walkers or those with extra days to spare might like to consider starting at East Linton or Dunbar and doing the John Muir Way to warm up and test equipment before the wilder parts are attempted. This arrangement means that the same railway line can be used (in conjunction with local buses) for access to the start and finish of your walk, wheras access by rail (and bus) from England to Portpatrick for the west end of the Southern Upland Way is more difficult and expensive.

A TRAIL AROUND THE SOUTH LANARKSHIRE BASTLE HOUSES

For those with a historical bent and an ability to cover thirty miles of very strenuous walking, including sections totalling five miles where there is not much of a path actually marked on the ground, this offers a fine two day adventure. Using a base at either Wanlockhead or Leadhills the circuit can be broken into two unequal circuits of about ten and twenty two miles. Those with three or four days available could use the station at Sanquhar as a starting point, or start from Beattock or Moffat.

BORDERS ABBEYS WAY

This 65m circular trail is mentioned in this book but is not described as such. It is adequately described in a set of five leaflets available from local tourist offices. The sections are: Hawick - Selkirk 12m, Selkirk - Melrose Abbey 10m, Melrose to Kelso Abbey via Dryburgh Abbey 18m, Kelso to Jedburgh Abbey 12m, and Jedburgh to Hawick 13m.

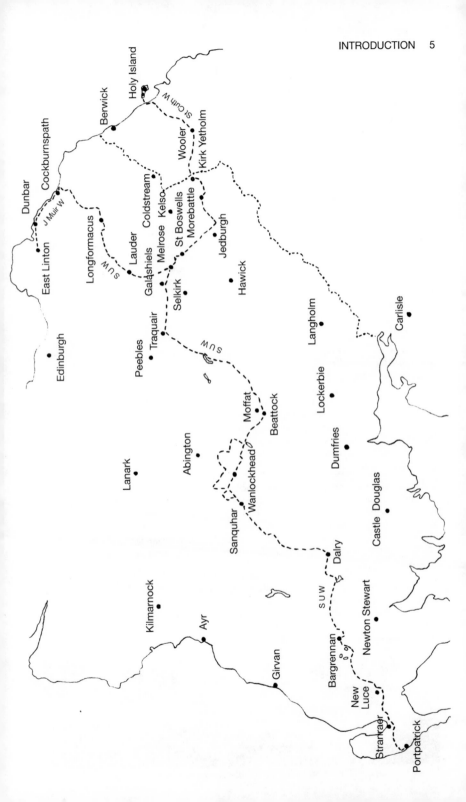

EQUIPMENT

1. MAPS

Walking the full length of the Southern Upland Way requires eight Ordnance Survey 1:50,000 scale Landranger Maps (82, 76, 77, 78, 79, 73, 74, and 67. Sheet 67 additionally covers the John Muir Way. Just sheet 78 alone will be adequate for the bastles trail, with or without extensions to or from Sanquhar or Beattock, although the bastle at Snar actually lies right at the bottom edge of sheet 72. The St Cuthbert's Way requires sheets 73, 74 and 75, although only the last is additional to what is needed for the Southern Upland Way. Don't rely on buying maps as you go since they will only be available in a very few places. The maps weigh 100g each so those doing all of the Southern Upland Way in one go may find it worth while posting the first five maps home from Galashiels or Melrose. It is a good idea to have a waterproof case to carry a map or two, plus this book and any other notes so you can check things even in wet and windy conditions.

2. NAVIGATIONAL AIDS

A particularly useful item is a Global Positioning System. You can check your speed and distance, and time travelled, but best of all it will give you a grid reference accurate to a few feet. This is very useful on mist-covered open moorlands. A GPS unit tends to use up batteries fairly quickly, so don't leave it on all day. It needs a clear view of the sky to function properly so although it will be alright on wide tracks in forests you will lose the signal if you venture in amongst densely packed trees.

Those who like treasure hunting can additionally use the unit to find geocaches (website details given on page 46), of which there are several along the routes.

3. FOOTWEAR

You will need a good pair of boots if walking the whole of the Southern Upland Way. Make sure they are worn in, but not so worn so that they will not last well over 200 miles. Along the way Moffat and Galashiels are the only places where you are likely to get new boots. It may be worth carrying a pair of trekking sandals, although they will weigh about 600g. These may be useful for fording any burns swollen by heavy rain, and in hot weather they may also be used for some sections on roads and tracks where the surfaces are good and ankle-support is less important. They will also be useful for indoors if you are planning to use bed and breakfast places and hotels. Carry enough socks to last three days, just in case wet weather delays drying times.

4. TREKKING POLES

Use of a pair of trekking poles is recommended. They enable the arms to do much of the work of propelling you forwards, especially on steep climbs. Having two means that you can use them as crutches if you hurt a leg or an ankle in a remote place and can't summon any assistance. Campers can save weight by carrying a tent or tarp which uses trekking poles for uprights such as the Mountain Equipment Ultralite. Trekking poles are useful for getting over stiles, fording streams, and pushing vegetation out of the way.

5. MEDICAL KIT

This should contain both ordinary plasters and ones designed specifically for blisters on your feet. You should also have a bandage, safety pins, antiseptic cream, general-purpose painkillers, cloves or Bonjela (for toothache), and medication for diarrhoea such as Imodium. You are also likely to need an ointment for muscular aches such as Ibuleve or Deep Heat. Vaseline is useful to rub onto sore feet,.

The Elidon Hills near Melrose, viewed from the east.

OTHER GENERAL ITEMS OF EQUIPMENT

Emergency Blanket: Silver foil cover to keep you warm in case of fall in a remote place.
Gaiters: Keeps your legs and feet dry when walkiing through long grass or mud.
Insect Repellant: Essential after the midge season starts in early June in Scotland.
Mirror: You may be able to save weight by carrying a combined mirror and hair-brush.
Mobile Phone: Essential for emergencies and making accommodation bookings, etc.
    You may not be able to get a signal in some places in the Southern Uplands.
Rucksack Cover: Use either a rucksack inner liner or outer cover, or both.
Sewing Kit: Suitable threads for repairs to clothing, rucksack, tent, etc.
    A small roll of cloth-backed tape is also useful for all kinds of repair jobs..
Toilet Paper: You should also carry a light trowel for burying used paper & excrement.
Toiletries: Carry small quantities of soaps & shampoos in old film containers, etc.
Towel: Use a special lightweight camping towel for minimal space and weight.
Umbrella: Of little use on exposed ridges, but useful on sheltered woodland paths.
Utensils: You'll need these sooner or later even if not camping.
Water Bottles: Try using a pair of one litre Platypus bottles, which go flat when empty.
Whistle: Traditional means of summoning help in case of an accident.
Writing Equipment: Pens, highlighter to mark map, ruler to measure mileages on map.
You may also want to carry a camera, binoculars, hat, gloves, swimming costume, torch, scissors. Campers will also need: Sleeping Bag, Inflatable Mat, Stove, Cooking Pans, Cup, Matches, Clothes Pegs, Pan Scrubber.

WEIGHT SAVING HINTS, PARTICULARLY FOR CAMPERS

    Weigh everything that goes in your pack. Leave behind all non-essentials and find lighter alternatives wherever possible. It really is worth it, you may be carrying this pack for over a fortnight. Carry just a few light items of clothing and wash them if necessary. so make sure they are quick drying. Use clothes with a proper wicking system, rather than your favourite old T-shirts and sweatshirts. The extra expense is worth it.

    Wearing waterproof clothing (eg the Paramo ranges) saves having to carry extra spare clothes and waterproofs in your pack. It also saves opening the pack to find waterproofs when it starts to rain. This sort of clothing may be too warm in high summer, although the trousers have side vents and jackets can be worn tied around the waist instead of in your pack. Most of the time only a single baselayer is needed under the jackets when you are walking with a pack on, but carry extra layers as needed.

    Try not to carry tins, The contents will often weigh 450g,the empty tin alone 70g, and you may have to carry the empty tin a long way until you see a rubbish bin. Consider buying a dehydrator. Dried foods will last several weeks, weigh very little, and can be carried in small plastic bags weighing nothing. You could post parcels of dried food ahead to post offices, hostels or any friends you are planning to stay with. Buying packets of ready dried meals from outdoor shops is very expensive and not recommended

    Try carrying items that are heavy, valuable or likely to be needed quickly (such as drinks, snacks, camera and binoculars) on a waist-belt or in a bum-bag across your chest rather than in your main pack. Check carefully that this is robust & comfortable.

    Meths is cheaper, easier to obtain, and lighter than gas canisters (the canisters alone weigh 65g). Remember though that meths stoves are a bit slower and not so safe to use within the confines of a porch of a tent. Never cook inside the main tent itself.

    Post home all surplus maps and guides, souvenirs purchased en route, and any items of equipment that prove to be superfluous. The weight saving really is worth the cost and trouble and the items are more likely to get damaged in your pack than in the post.

    Try to keep your total pack weight under 9kg (roughly 20lbs) not including food, water and fuel. Its possible to get this weight down to 5 or 6kg for weekend trips, but when walking for more than a few days you may need more clothes and socks, a deodorant, swimming costume, sandals, more maps and guides, shaving gear, and other extra items which will increase the weight of your pack. Food for a whole day will normally weigh almost 1kg, especially if you carry bread, but using Ryvitas, oatcakes and dried foods may reduce this to about 750g per day. Even when using dried foods enough supplies to give a safety margin in case of delay for a seven day trek away from all shops will weigh over 5kg, so your pack could then weigh at least 14kg (37lbs) in total.

OUTDOOR SAFETY

Make sure you are wearing footwear suitable for the nature of the terrain and that you have enough dry clothes to remain warm enough even in the most stormy conditions. Always carry an emergency blanket to keep the body warm enough in case of an accident. Stop and sort out any problems with your feet or boots immediately. When walking on roads face the oncoming traffic, ie the righthand side of the road.

Even on well signed paths it's important to keep note of where you are on the map. If you need help you may need to be able to give a grid reference quickly in order for emergency services to arrive promptly. If you have to leave someone in order to get help try to make sure they have enough food and drink for several hours and that they will be warm enough. Carry enough food and drink so that you don't have to rush unduly or take risks or dodgy shortcuts. Running down slopes can cause erosion and is more likely to lead to accidents. Don't drink water or eat any foodstuffs gathered or found by the wayside unless you are sure it is safe to do so.

Be realistic when estimating times and distances. Very few people can walk at more than three miles an hour for any period of time even on a straight and level road or track. On rocky, meandering river-side paths criss-crossed by tree-roots or on steep uphill sections of path distances will be further than they appear to be on an Ordnance Survey map and you are not likely to do much more than two miles an hour, including short stops. Even for strong walkers on comparatively easy terrain twenty miles will usually take eight hours to cover, including short stops, and the 26 mile section lacking shops or bed and breakfast places between St John's Town of Dalry and Sanquhar is unlikely to be covered in less than eleven hours. A two and a half mile section on boggy moorland where there's little obvious path, necessitating frequent stops to check the map or GPS could take two hours in bad weather conditions and add an extra hour to your estimated time of arrival. Remember that you may need to allow some time for jobs such as washing and wringing out clothing, shopping and maintaining your equipment.

ENVIRONMENTAL IMPACT

Basically: Leave nothing but footprints, take nothing but photographs & memories. So:
Don't leave any litter, even biodegradable material such as fruit cores and skins.
Don't pick flowers or damage trees & plants, except where necessary to clear a path.
Don't make lots of unecessary noise, especially when passing through farmyards.
Don't get so close to animals that they become stressed and abandon their young.
Don't stray from the right of way, assuming, of course, you can clearly see its route.
Don't touch farming or forestry equipment, crops, timber stacks or building materials.
Leave all gates as you find them, whether open or closed..
Be discreet if wild camping (see page 10), and guard against all risk of accidental fires.

Use public toilets where possible. When you have to go outdoors make sure you are at least 30m from running water and bury excrement in a small hole where it will decompose quicker. Do not bury tampons or sanitary towels. You will have to carry these out. Ideally you should also do this with toilet paper also, since it doesn't decompose quickly and will blow around if dug up by animals.

Try to support local businesses where possible. This puts money into the pockets of local people who keep the countryside running, rather than making profits for huge urban-based corporations.

Dogs are prohibited from some sections of both the Southern Upland Way and the St Cuthbert's Way which are on paths which permissive rather than rights of way. Both these routes traverse moors where wild birds breed at ground level and fields may contain ewes with lambs. Dogs should not be allowed to interfere with either birds or ewes, and you can expect justifiable hostility from farmers if using the ways with a dog in the lambing season. Also be careful to keep dogs away from cattle. Dog owners will also have to think carefully about where they can stay. On the John Muir Way there are not likely to be problems with dogs encountering livestock but owners will need to remove all dog mess and keep their dogs away from any small children using the beaches.

ACCESS TO THE WAYS

Portpatrick is not the easiest of places to get to by public transport from England. Buses to and from Stranraer are hourly at times, and there are occasional busses from there to other places on or near the Way such as Castle Kennedy and Glenluce, but the problem is getting to Stranraer from anywhere in Scotland or England. There are about six trains daily from Glasgow taking nearly three hours. Access from England will usually involve changing trains at Carlisle (itself three hours travel from Leeds or Birmingham) and again at Kilmarnock, although there is currently one direct evening train from Newcastle upon Tyne via Carlisle. There is, however, an overnight coach service from Birmingham to Belfast that not only serves Stranraer and several places in Northern England, but other places in Galloway south of the Way such Castle Douglas, which has buses to Ayr via Dalry, and Newton Stewart, which has buses connecting it with Girvan via Bargrennan.

Apart from Stranraer, where the station is two miles from the nearest point of the Way, Sanquhar is the only place where the Southern Upland Way crosses a railway near a station and the service is rarely more frequent than a train each way to Glasgow or Dumfries every two hours. Sanquhar has a few buses to Wanlockhead and Leadhills and more frequent ones to Kilmarmock and Dumfries. Beatoock and Moffat have reasonable bus connections with Edinburgh and Glasgow, and southwards to the stations at Lockerbie and Carlisle. St Mary's Loch has very few buses but Traquair has a few to Peebles. Although Galashiels and Melrose have lost their rail services there are hourly buses to Peebles, Edinburgh, Hawick, Berwick, Carlisle, and to places on or near St Cuthbert's Way and the Borders Abbeys Way such as Jedburgh. Further east on that route Kirk Yetholm has a few buses, and Wooler is served by Newcastle to Coldstream services,

Lauder is served by buses between Edinburgh and Coldstream and Berwick. On weekdays Cockburnspath is served by six buses a day in each direction between Edinburgh and Berwick, and these buses also serve East Linton, Dunbar and Innerwick for access onto the John Muir Way They also call at Coldingham (where there's a youth hostel) and Eyemouth. Dunbar has trains running between Edinburgh and Birmingham but a change at Newcastle is usually required for access to and from London. Some trains stop at Berwick, and from there buses run three times a day onto Holy Island, although their times rotate according to when the tidal causeway is passable.

Mining remains near Wanlockhead

SERVICES ON THE WAYS

The Southern Upland Way and the St Cuthbert's Way do not pass close to any outdoor equipment shops selling anything much other than clothing, although campers may at least be able to obtain fuel in Stranraer, Sanquhar, Moffar, Galashiells, Melrose, Jedburgh and Wooler, whilst a souvenir shop in Portpatrick sells walking sticks. Food and bed and breakfast accommodation can be obtained in all these places, and also near Castle Kennedy and at Bargrennan, Dalry, Leadhills, Lauder and Cockburnspath on the Southern Upland Way, and at St Boswells and Morebattle on St Cuthbert's Way, whilst the town of Jedburgh lies not far off the route of the latter. Note that some B&B places may be willing to collect or drop walkers at road-accessible points on the ways a few miles from their location - see the Southern Upland Way accomodation leaflet.

HOSTELS, BOTHIES AND CAMPING

On the Southern Upland Way only Portpatrick, Sanquhar, Beattock, and Lauder now have campsites and the only youth hostels are Kendoon, Broadmeadows, and Melrose, plus Minnigaff and Coldingham lying considerably off the route. The St Cuthbert's Way is served by a SHYA hostel at Kirk Yetholm and a YHA hostel at Wooler, and there are campsites at Ancrum and Wooler. However there are six open shelters (bothies) lying beside or close to the western and middle sections of the Southern Upland Way. From west to east these are at Laggangarn, White Laggan, Polskeith, Brattleburn, Over Phawhope and Minch Moor. None have any facilities or equipment, and all bedding and comforts have to be carried in, and all rubbish carried out. Laggangairn and Minch Moor are small single-room wooden cabins without any means of heating but the other four are larger and have stoves or fireplaces in the main rooms. In each case water is obtained from nearby streams and users need to be careful not to pollute these streams in any way.

Camping out in wild places without any facilities is great fun, saves money and will save having to make any diversions off the routes. Obtain prior verbal permission from landowners for camping if possible. It is unlikely you'll be arrested for camping anywhere, unless you are causing damage, an obstruction, or some other serious nuisance, but you could be moved on. It is legal to stop for rest or refreshment whilst walking along a right-of-way but there is no right to erect any sort of shelter, however temporary. Note that camping is strictly forbidden on Holy Island because it is a wildlife sanctuary.

The basic rule about wild camping is to be discreet. Use a tent with a flysheet of a colour that blends with its surroundings, and (except in very remote or secluded places) pitch fairly late, leave early, and don't light fires anywhere near trees. Don't leave rubbish, make noise, or pitch close to, or within sight of, roads or houses, or in fields containing animals, especially cows. Finding places to wild camp isn't always easy as much of the terrain will be too steep, too rough, or boggy, or overgrown or overlooked. Also, finding shelter from the wind and any drinkable water can be a problem on some sections. Do not drink water that's run over arable land possibly treated with chemicals, or which may have been polluted by cattle or drainage from buildings. On the final fifth of the Southern Upland Way between Melrose and Cockburnspath there are no toilets except at Lauder and the streams are comparatively low lying and likely to be polluted by animals.

SOUVENIR MERKS AND OTHER THINGS TO FIND

When the Southern Upland Way was improved in 2004, local artists got together and created a series of kists in which placed waymerks, which are small hand-made coins of copper or lead, for walkers to collect as souvenirs. Still kept occasionally topped up by the wardens, the kists are not that obvious and lie in fairly remote locations. You can tell if there is a kist ahead by looking out for tiny plaques on the waymarking posts on which appears the word Ultreia, meaning "on with your quest". If you pass a second post with such a plaque then you have missed the kist between the two posts.

Remember that there are geocaches to be found on all of the ways, especially the John Muir Way, if you have a GPS unit (see note on geocaching on page 6.

Also the author has hidden several disks bearing the names of castles on and around the trails east of Moffat. Finding them entitles you to free or reduced price books.See the treasure trail page on the Folly Publications website (details inside back of cover).

Bridge over River Tweed connecting St Cuthbert's Way with Dryburgh Abbey

WALKING CONDITIONS

Ordinary shoes will be adequate for the John Muir Way, which is comparatively level and does not cross any bogs. Only the last mile into Dunbar is road, and there is beach walking as an alternative, but a mile section around Torness Power Station is on concrete. About 16m of St Cuthbert's Way is on roads, but there is a beach alternative for four miles onto Holy Island. Only the Morebattle to Wooler section requires footwear suitable for mountain walking. The bastles trail is a tough walk with a lot of climbing and sections of up to three miles over exposed moors with only a hint of a path. It requires good hill-walking equipment and navigational skills. Only four miles of it is on tarmac roads.

The 212m Southern Upland Way requires the best possible footwear and equipment. There are lengthy moorland sections which are boggy in places. In all there are 43 miles on mostly quiet roads. Between New Luce and Ettrick Head there are about 40 miles in total in conifer plantations, partly on forest tracks and partly on paths through grass.

Cove Harbour from the clifftop path near Cockburnspath

THE SOUTHERN UPLAND WAY

PORTPATRICK - WATER OF LUCE

Portpatrick is named after the patron saint of Ireland, which lies just 22m away. From 1622 there was weekly mail ferry from here to Donaghadee, and a trade in cattle and horses grew up after a pier was built at Portpatrick in 1774. A frequent paddle-boat mail service was established after completion of an artificial harbour costing half a million pounds begun in 1821. However, it proved too exposed to the prevailing SW winds and after the service was transferred to Straraer in the 1860s Portpatrick became a sleepy holiday village. It is now dominated by a large cliff-top Victorian hotel and only has a few small shops. There is a ruined cruciform church of 1629 with a circular 16th century west tower with a conical top. Half a mile SE of the village is a campsite and the path connecting the two uses a section of the trackbed of the railway that once served the port. This section of the railway lies on the clifftops and here is the spectacularly sited ruin of Dunskey Castle, seat of the Adair family until sold to the Montgomeries in 1620. Although parts of the wall cutting off the promontory may be older, most of it is late 16th century and during that period the abbot of Saulseat Abbey nearby to the NE was confined and tortured here in an attempt to make him sign away the lands of the abbey.

A sign marks the begining of the Southern Upland Way by the harbour. The path heads NW up onto a cliff with several masts. In spring look out here for thrift (pink flowers) and spring squill (blue flowers and curly leaves). In just under a mile there are steps down to the the first of two small inlets, Port Mora and Port Kale, with a short climb between them and a longer climb after the second to regain the top of the 160ft high cliffs. Just short of the second mile there's another gully to cross. After two and half miles the Way joins the road running out to the lighthouse on Blackhead and turns inland to meet and go left along A764 for a short way. Four miles from Portpatrick turn right onto a lane for a mile. Turn sharp right back on yourself on a farm tack that heads south then east. After 500yards the way becomes a path going straight on over a hillock and then across the north side of Broad Moor with views of a small loch to the north. Only posts mark this section of about two thirds of a mile across moorland and it is easy to veer off the route in misty conditions. Turn right to descend on a road from the end of loch towards Stranraer. The road crosses two streams with slight rises after each. The T-junction after the second is eight miles from Portpatrick. The Way goes right but turn left for the quickest and quietest way into Stranraer, where the shops are just over a mile away, although its two miles to the station, which lies close to where the car-ferries depart for Larne in Northern Ireland. Stranraer offers all the services you are likely to need except that there is no proper outdoor equipment shop, one having recently closed in 2005. The only tourist attraction is the Castle of St John, a L-plan tower built by the Adairs c1510. It was given an extra storey c1600 and remodelled as the town gaol in the early 19th century.

Portpatrick

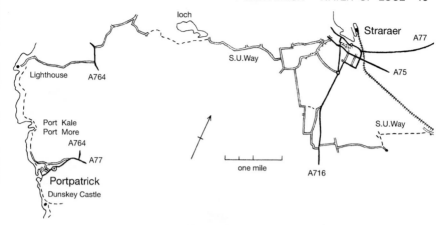

Turning right at the T-junction above Stranraer soon brings the Way to a backroad to Portpatrick. Turn left towards Stranraer and then right onto a lane. At the double bend in half a mile either carry on along the lane and turn right to reach A716, or take the path down across a field from the second bend to turn right onto the lane to the A716. Go left a few yards on the main road then right along a lane, passing a barn on the right. Turn right onto another lane, then left on a lane up to Culhorn Mains. Go left just before the farm, and keep right to go along a straight level track passing a small lochan in woods on the left. Turn right on a road and at a T-junction go under the railway bridge and take a path on the right through a belt of trees on the north side of the line. At a housing estate go right (almost straight on), then turn left and cross over A75 onto a track leading along the SE end of the White Loch. Alternatively, turning right for just a few yards down the main road gives access to a petrol station with a water tap and shop.

The track eventually bends round right to meet a lane after passing the entrance to Castle Kennedy, (14m from Portpatrick), a tall building erected c1600 by John Kennedy, 5th Earl of Cassuillis. The site, now delightful gardens on a penninsular between the White and Black Lochs, was then a small island in the middle of a single lake and had been occupied by a castle since the late 15th century. It was sold to the Dalrymples of Stair in 1674 and has been a ruin since an accidental fire in 1716, being superseded by Lochinch Castle of the 1860s half a mile further north.

Turn left onto the road for half a mile until just before a right-hand bend there is a lane on the right leading past a few buildings to a half mile long section of path climbing up through a field before it rejoins the road. Turn right and then in 300yards right again onto a track leading up into a forest. The Way original stayed on the track for over a mile but it now turns left onto a new path which winds around near the forest edge along the south side of the Craig Burn. It only regains the original route two miles further on where it comes alongside the railway in a thin belt of trees. Eventually the path goes under the railway and doubles back southwards to a new bridge over the Water of Luce.

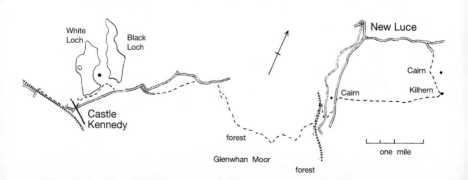

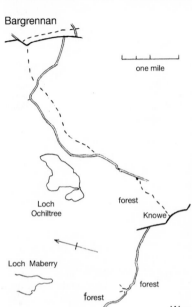

Laggangarn Standing Stones

From the bridge over the Water of Luce the Way climbs up to go left on a road for 180yards and then, almost opposite Cairn MacNeilie in a field on the left, turns right along a track for a mile and a half out to the ruined farm of Kilhern. One building has enough roof left to give walkers some shelter for a short break. The track turns north for a mile, passing close to the west of a chambered long cairn at NX 199644 called the Caves of Kilhern, and meeting the New Luce to Tarf Bridge road near a waterfall on the Cross Water of Luce. A shorter and easier alternative to going via Kilhern is to stay on the road to New Luce, which has a shop and a pub that allows camping, turning right there onto the road to the waterfall. Follow the unfenced road eastwards for 400 yards before forking left for a mile up to Balmurrie. On approaching another farm not far beyond the Way now takes the track up towards Kilmacfadzean for 250yards before striking right across rough moorland. For a mile there's not much path as such so you'll be relying on the marker posts or your navigational skills to get you to where a path enters the forest at NX 214687. East of the route are a pair of hut-circles and the long burial cairn of Cairn na Gath at NX 212674.

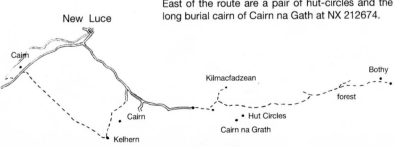

Pentagonal bothy at Laggangarn

In the forest the path crosses to meet a track, on which turn right for half a mile before forking right onto a path leading past the pentagonal wooden open bothy of Laggangarn at NX 221714 in a clearing traversed by a small burn. The standing stones incised with 6th or 7th century crosses lie a little further on at NX 222716, just before crossing Tarf Water. Still in forest the path climbs up to a cairn, just before which is a sign pointing to the Wells of the Rees, three drystone domed structures three feet high over springs.From the cairn the path goes along the the SE flank of Craig Ailie Fell. Drop down to the right to find a second parallel path leading to a forestry track at NX 240737. Turn right along the track and after half a mile a sign points across 600yards of rough pathless moor to Linn's Tomb, a small walled enclosure with plaques commemorating the shepherd Alexander Linn, a Covenanter shot by dragoons in this vicinity. Carry along the track to pass Derry, beyond which there is a short stretch without trees. After another mile in forest turn right and the track becomes a tarmac road at Darloskine Bridge, Follow the road for two miles to turn right heading SE on B7027 to Knowe.

At Knowe turn left on a path through forest for a mile to meet a road near Glenruther Lodge. Turn left down the road. You can follow the road for four miles to A714 but the Way itself goes over the western peak of Glenvernoch Fell just east of the road, and a new off-road section now extends across its northern flank, saving two miles and,f of road walking, although the going isn't that easy either underfoot or navigationally speaking. The Way originally cut across to go through Bargrennan, which has a shop, pub and camp-site, and then followed a path eastwards through forest to Minniwick, However its now been re-routed along a path on the SW fringe of forest, close to the River Cree, and if you don't need the services in Bargrennan one option is to continue down the road, turn right along A714 for a short distance, and then cross the river on a lane heading heading NE towards Minniwick. Once over the bridge follow the Way to the right. It bends round, goes left for a few yards on a road, then takes a track off right. After half a mile a new forest path leaving on the right follows the Water of Trool (except for cutting off one bend) round to where a track crosses the river on a bridge SE of Minniwick, 43m from Portpatrick.

Loch Trool

one mile

Caldons

forest

forest

Minniwick

forest

forest

Bargrennan

After crossing the Water of Trool on the track serving Holm the Way takes the form of a path along the south side of the river. There is a seat almost opposite where the Water of Minnoch joins from the north. After two and a half miles from the bridge the path passes close to the Martyr's Tomb, a walled enclosure with a plaque commemorating six Covenanters who were shot after being caught by surprise at prayer. The Way then crosses a track over the river on another bridge. It gave access to Caldons campsite, now gone, not even a water tap now remaining. The path then runs through woods on the south side of Loch Trool and there's quite a bit of up and down and twisting and turning on this two mile section leading to where Robert the Bruce won his first battle against the English in 1307. The Way originally stayed south of the Glenhead Burn on a path leading to a forest track made in the 1970s (now a cycleway). It now crosses the burn, follows its northen bank for 400yards until well past Glenhead, and then cuts up across rough ground and regains the track at NX 449787. After one more mile the track does a sweep southwards away from the west end of Loch Dee, and a track climbing southwards from it to Drigmorn passes after 300yards the bothy of White Laggan. A second former farmstead, Black Laggan, is now only a ruin.

Half a mile north of Black Laggan the track passes a seat with a view of Loch Dee. After two more miles turn left at a junction of tracks to cross the River Dee, and then go right for three more miles to where there is a cycle-track mileage marker above the northern edge of Clatteringshaws Loch. There is a visitor centre near where Bruce won another skirmish with English forces in 1307 on the east side of the loch, but this lies over two miles off the Way, which turns north beyond the cycle-track mileage marker. On finding a road in a narrow belt of clear land in the forests turn left and then after 300yards take a path on the right across the clearing and into a mile wide belt of forest beyond. The Way runs along the SE flank of Shield Rig for over a mile. At Clenrie it turns right on a track which after a mile becomes a road which is followed for two and half miles until at NX 598820 a path leaves on the left. It crosses the Coom Burn and climbs over the south flank of Waterside Hill, passing close to a circular trench called The Score at NX 605816 which is said to mark the spot where a reveller from Dalry escaped the clutches of witches by marking a circle with his sword, although they cut off his horse's tail hanging over the line. The story is said to have inspired Robert Burns' Tam o Shanter. The path drops 200ft to cross A762 near a power station and then runs along the west bank of the Water of Ken to where there is a footbridge below Dalry, 64m from Portpatrick

Battle monument on north side of Loch Trool

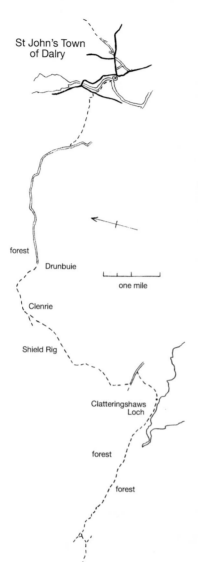

St John's Town
of Dalry

forest

Drunbuie

one mile

Clenrie

Shield Rig

Clatteringshaws
Loch

forest

forest

Old burial aisle in Dalry kirkyard

On the other bank, above the footbridge lies the church of Dalry dating from 1829. The village derives its full name of St John's Town of Dalry from a former medieval church here with that dedication. The only relic of it is what was a south transeptal burial aisle built to contain the remains of Sir James Gordon, killed in the battle of Pinkie in 1547, and his wife Margaret Gordon. North of the church is a 12th century castle mound or motte. There are toilets in the grounds of a chapel facing the junction of A713 and A702 and as you walk east down the latter there's a couple of shops. There are no suitable camping places between Shield Rig and Dalry and nothing beyond either for three miles but the farmer at Newfield Farm south of the road junction occasionally allows backpackers to pitch in a field opposite the hotel. A water tap is the only facility.

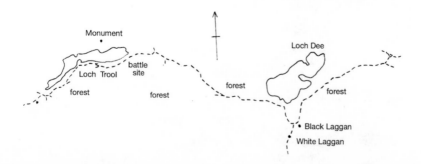

Monument

Loch Dee

battle
site

Loch Trool

forest

forest

forest

forest

forest

Black Laggan

White Laggan

Not far beyond a cross-roads at the east end of Dalry the Way follows a lane off to the left. this leads to a path heading north to Ardoch. Another path off to the right of the track from the farm continues heading north round the east side of Ardoch Hill. The Way climbs to the left a mile after coming alongside a forest but is not well marked at this point. If you miss it simply follow the forest edge to a road and turn left to regain the Way at the road junction at NX 637868. There are hut circles and other ancient remains between the line of the Way and the road. At the junction take the right fork heading north from there and then after a mile go left up Culmark Hill 350yards beyond the Butterhole Bridge over Black Water. A diversionary path follows the north bank of the burn for a mile and a half off the Way to the youth hostel of Kendoon beside B7000. After a mile from the road the Way descends to use the Culmark farmtrack which passes the Stroanfreggan Cairn shortly after a bridge over Stroanfreggan Burn. A flint knife was found in a sealed stone kist in the 25m diameter pile of stones.

Beyond the cairn turn right onto the unfenced B729 for 200yards, then take a path leading left off the track off left up to Stroanpatrick. Humps and bumps of an older farm marked also by a single tree will be passed as you climb and to the west of the newer farm a fort with two concentric rings of drystone walls can be seen on a crag. The path eventually enters forestry surrounding the summit of Manquhill Hill. The Way actually goes over the top but easier progress can be made along either of the forest tracks on the west and east flanks. Using the latter is a longer way and involves losing 200ft of height that has to be regained but allows sheltering in a bird-watching hide at NX 668942. Manquhill just to the north of it used to be an open bothy but was locked by the owners three years ago because of misuse. From where the tracks and the Way over the top come together again at NX 666956 either follow the ill-defined Way or use a dead-end forest track round the bend to NX 669959 and then take the path heading north and then NE to climb 650ft in a mile to the 1940ft high summit of Benbrack.

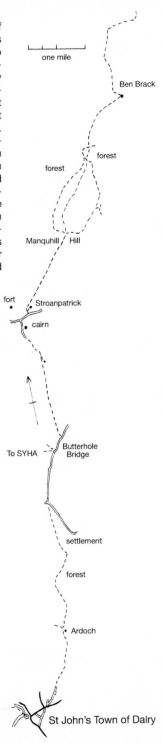

Interior of Chalk Memorial Bothy, Polskeith

On the top of Benbrack the path bends tightly back to the left and follows the fence (a real help in misty conditions) along an undulating ridge to Cairn Hill and then east to Black Hill. The Way then enters the western edge of forestry and at High Countam becomes a forest track. Cross over another forest track on a path out to Allan's Cairn, a sandstone memorial to George Allan and Margaret Gracie, two Covenanters shot in this vicinity. The path eventually bends to the left to join the forest track crossed earlier to head north descending beside a burn.After a hairpin left-hand bend it passes the single room Chalk Memorial bothy, 81m from Portpatrick, which in June 2005 was the best furnished bothy ever to be seen.

The track turns right where a path joins just after the bothy and then in 200yards keep right at the junction of tracks to gain a road at Polskeith. Follow the road for just over two miles to Polgown and then go left, climbing 500ft in a mile and a half to go over Cloud Hill. Over the next three miles the route gradually becomes a more obvious path as it descends 1100ft. Eventually a track, it meets a road at Ulzieside. Go left and cross Euchan Water, and go right at a cross-roads over the River Nith. Then take a river-bank path on the right along the south side of the small town of Sanquhar. Where the Way turns left along A76 there is a petrol station with a small camp-site, 90m from Portpatrick. At the corner before this are the castle ruins, once freely accessible but now fenced off. It was a seat of the Crichtons until sold in 1639 to Sir William Douglas of Drumlanrig, later 1st Earl of Queensberry. The isolated square tower at the south corner dates from c1360 and the half-round tower and adjoining gateway are mid 15th century. Just west of where the Way heads off north from A76 are a Co-op and several other shops, plus the 18th century tolbooth, beyond which a lane leads off to the station.

Sanquhar Castle

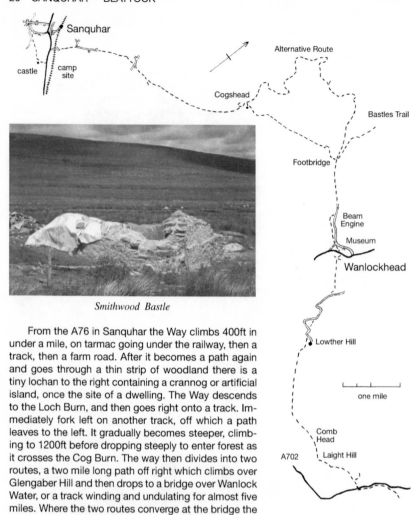

Smithwood Bastle

From the A76 in Sanquhar the Way climbs 400ft in under a mile, on tarmac going under the railway, then a track, then a farm road. After it becomes a path again and goes through a thin strip of woodland there is a tiny lochan to the right containing a crannog or artificial island, once the site of a dwelling. The Way descends to the Loch Burn, and then goes right onto a track. Immediately fork left on another track, off which a path leaves to the left. It gradually becomes steeper, climbing to 1200ft before dropping steeply to enter forest as it crosses the Cog Burn. The way then divides into two routes, a two mile long path off right which climbs over Glengaber Hill and then drops to a bridge over Wanlock Water, or a track winding and undulating for almost five miles. Where the two routes converge at the bridge the bastles trail heads north over Reecleugh Hill and into Lanarkshire (see pages 42).

Follow the track along the north side of Wanlock Water past a cemetery. This whole valley is full of remains of lead mines and close to where the Way crosses to the south side of the burn is a beam engine for pumping water out of mine-shafts (see pictures on pages 2 & 9). The village of Wanlockhead elevated at about 1300ft lies just to the east but has little to offer apart from a mining museum, a simple church of 1848, and one or two b&b places. The youth hostel and shop have closed and the nearest shop is at Leadhills (in Lanarkshire) almost two miles north up the B797. Gold was mined here in the late 16th century but by the mid 18th century lead was the principal ore being mined, one shaft being so deep that it was 400ft below sea-level The last mines survived until 1914.

The Way crosses B797 to a track climbing to meet the road to the "golf ball" early warning establishment on the 2400ft high summit of Lowther Hill. Bits of path cut off the zig-zags of the road. The path continues along the ridge to Cold Moss and Comb Head, and then drops and climbs again to Laght Hill, by which time it has been on or near the Dumfriess-shire - Lanarkshire county boundary for three miles. Finally it plunges into Lanarkshire, dropping 600ft to pass Overfingland and cross over slight traces of a Roman Road and the A702.

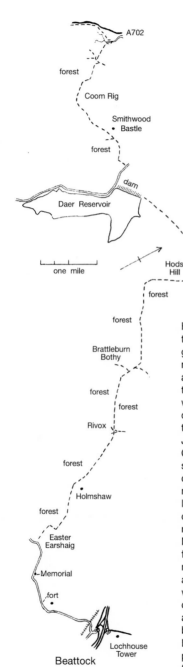

A702

forest

Coom Rig

Smithwood
• Bastle

forest

dam

Daer Reservoir

one mile

Hods
Hill

forest

forest

Brattleburn
Bothy

forest

forest

Rivox

forest

• Holmshaw

forest

Easter
Earshaig

Memorial

fort

Lochhouse
Tower

Beattock

The Way follows the east side of A702 for half a mile to Potrenick Burn and then takes a path on the right to cross a footbridge over Portrail Water. After following the river bank a short way southwards it enters a forest and turns left then immediately right on forest tracks. Just before a second forest on the side of Hitteril Hill is entered, two and a half miles from A702, a ruin is visible at NS 959093. This is the Smithwood Bastle (see page 45). In the forest turn left onto a road and then left to cross the dam of Daer Reservoir (until recently the route went further north here to drop below the dam and the maintenance buildings - the new route is easier and shorter). Cross a stile and follow the south side of the fence up to the summit of Hods Hill, 700ft above the Daer reservoir. The Way follows the outside of the forest fence until finally entering at NT 004080 and descending for over a mile in a wide fire-break. Just south of the crossing of tracks and a memorial to a shepherd who died here in a snowstorm at 020071 a signed path leads off west to Brattleburn Bothy.

Still in a wide fire-break the Way climbs over Craig Hill. Three miles after the bothy path the way leaves the fire-break, forking right into the forest and zigzagging to the road near Easter Earshaig. Passing another memorial to an unfortunate shepherd by the roadside at the edge of the forest, going below a fort on Beattock Hill, and past a farm just after the railway bridge which has a circular building which was once a horse-operated mill, follow the road for just over two miles to the Beattock House Hotel by junction 15 on A74(M). Just to the north is Old Brig Inn dating from 1821. Once having stables for fifty horses as an important staging post on the Carlisle to Glasgow road, it was designed by Thomas Telford, who also designed the nearby bridge over Evan Water dated 1819. The village of Beattock extending down the minor road south of there offers a camp site but there is no shop. If you need one follow A701 (pavement most of the way) into Moffat where a Co-op is hidden behind the Tourist Office, 119m from Portpatrick. The Ram Fountain in the middle is indicative of the importance of sheep trading and rearing in this area. Moffat was also a spa town with sulphur spring a mile to the north, said to be a cure for gout, skin diseases, rheumatism, and stomach problems. Baths and a new assembly room were built in the early 19th century. The road builder John Loudon McAdam is buried in the cemetery. The Way passes Dumcrieff, where he lived in the 1780s, to the SE of the town, and its next owner was Dr Currie, who wrote a biography of Robert Burns, a visitor to Moffat, where he wrote several poems. In Station Park is a memorial to Air Chief Marshal Dowding, who was in charge of Britain air defences in the Battle of Britain in 1940 and was born in Moffat.

THE SOUTHERN UPLAND WAY

BEATTOCK - DRYHOPE

From the hotel at the north end of Beattock a path between hedges leads to subways under A701 and A74(M). Turn right onto a road to a T-junction. On the left Lochhouse Tower is visible, a round-cornered early 16th century structure built by the Johnstones and restored in the 1990s. If you've taken the A701 into Moffat to get supplies you'll get a much closer look. At the T-junction there is a path over the hill opposite giving views of Moffat. Descend and turn left on a road, then turn right to cross over Moffat Water before taking a path on the left following the south bank through beech trees. Opposite lies Dumcrieff (see bottom of page 21). After two thirds of a mile cross a road onto a track and follow it to the right as it climbs. Hidden in woods beside the Cornal Burn 200yards to the left is the last remaining fragment of another 16th century Johnstone tower, together with footings of an outbuilding across the neck of the strong promontory site.

The track does a double bend and comes alongside the burn before entering the forest. Keep left at the next junction and cross the burn, pass close to Craighope Hope. After another mile take the path off left at a right-hand hairpin bend of the track as it crosses Wamphray Water. Rising beside the burn you will emerge from the forest to climb above the gorge of the Selcoth Burn (one of the best parts of the Way) and then cross it on the way up to the 1700ft high pass of Ettrick Head, 125m from Portpatrick, and the border between Dumfriesshire and the Selkirk district of Borders Region. It is also a watershed between east and west draining rivers. Descend slightly and keep right to find a good track, through forest at first, down to the bothy at Over Phawhope.

A mile beyond Over Phawhope the track becomes a road, followed for five miles to Scabcleugh. Halfway down this quiet road there are scots pines above a section of gorge at Nether Phawhope on the right and traces of a chapel and burial ground at Over Kirkhope on the left. The scots pines are a relic of the huge medieval Ettrick Forest, a royal hunting ground. Take the signed path climbing up left beside Scabcleugh Burn. This is a quite clear path higher up as it goes round the side of Peniestone Knowe, and descends to ruined Riskinhope Hope. It then climbs again on the side of Earl's Hill to turn left onto another signed path called the Captain's Road just before this in turn becomes a good track all the way down to the Tibbie Shiels Inn, 138m from Portpatrick and just over 20m from Beattock. The pub offers accomodation and camping and is named after its first proprietor. Here a shepherd poet, James Hogg, 1770 - 1835, began his friendship with the novelist Sir Walter Scott. Both Hogg and Tibbie (and her husband) were buried in Ettrick churchyard, which lies a mile further down the valley from the turn-off at Scabcleugh. It's possible to go that way and cut back to the Way on another path, although there is a one mile section of this other path that is boggy and hard to follow.

Scabcleugh

Brockhoperig

Crook Cottage

Nether Phawhope

Broadgairhill

Potburn

Over Phawhope

forest

Ettrick Head

Selcoth Burn

forest

forest

one mile

forest

Craigbeck Hope

forest

Cornal Tower

A708

Dumcrieff

Moffat

A701

Lochhouse Tower

Beattock

A74(M)

Monument to James Hogg

The track continues past the pub to the A708, where there is a cafe and toilets, plus a monument to James Hogg at this popular beauty spot between St Mary's Loch and the Loch of the Lowes. Originally they were one lake but silt brought down by burns has created deltas between them. At the pub the Way was officially opened in April 1984, and it takes a path through a sailing club grounds and along the SE side of St Mary's Loch. Beyond Bowerthorpe the path becomes a track flanked by woodland. Across the loch from here four trees mark where there was a chapel in which William Wallace is said to have been made Warden of Scotland in 1297. In the 17th century Covenanting ministers are said to have preached in the ruins with just a blanket to protect them from the weather. After it crosses a bridge over Yarrow Water issuing from the loch a path on the right leads through to A708. Cross over and go up to a track, to the left of which is 16th century Dryhope Tower, (cover picture) now conserved as a ruin, although since it has a top vault it can offer brief shelter to walkers. It was the birthplace in 1550 of Mary Scott, the famous "Flower of Yarrow" of the Border ballads. She is said to have once served up to her husband "Auld Wat" of Harden a dish of a pair of riding spurs as a reminder that the larder was empty and that he needed to go and steal some cattle. A datestone of 1613 has initials of a later Mary Scott and her husband Philip who restored the tower after James VI had had it dismantled because "Auld Wat" was involved in a rebellion.

Blackhouse Tower

About 350 yards beyond the tower take the path off on the right for two miles across to Blackhouse, where James Hogg was a sheherd for ten years. It was his friendship with the owner's son William Laidlaw that led to his association with Sir Walter Scott. Near the house are remains of another 16th century tower, which belonged to the Stewarts of Traquair. This building has a circular stair turret at one corner, possibly a later addition and a rare feature amongst the many towers in this area. Cross over the track up to Blackhouse and follow a faint path first through forestry for a mile and then a good track over Blake Muir. Descend past the end of a belt of spruce trees, cross two fields onto a track down to B709 and turn left along it for a mile, passing Traquair Church of 1778, to the crossroads at Traquair, 150m from Portpatrick. The Way turns right but if you need a shop, accommodation or a campsite you will have to carry on along the B709 for another mile and half into Innerleithen. Half a mile north of the crossroads is Traquair House, a 16th century mansion of Stewarts on the site of a royal hunting lodge later held by the Murray family. Opening onto B7062 are the Bear Gates, closed since at least 1745.

Traquair House

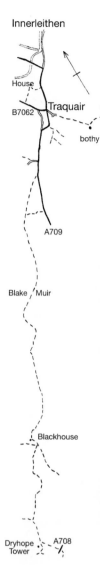

Innerleithen

one mile

House

Traquair

B7062

Cheese Well

Minch Moor

bothy

A709

Blake Muir

Blackhouse

Dryhope   A708
Tower

cairn

Broomy Law

Brown
Knowe

Hare Law

To SYHA
Broadmeadows

Minch Moor Rd

From the war memorial by the crossroads in Traquair the Way heads SE on what starts as a road but beyond the school on the right it becomes a cobbled rack. Soon after entering forestry the log-cabin Minchmoor bothy appears on the right. Cross over two forest tracks and keep left when the path divides. It climbs to 1700ft on the flank of Minch Moor, passing a spring on the right called the Cheese Well. Traditionally travellers on this ancient trackway offered food to the spirits of the well. Shortly afterwards you will get a first glimpse of the twin peaks of the Eildon Hills SE of Melrose, which will be in view for most of the next thirty miles or so. Descending in a wide open belt through the forest, the path crosses a track and goes over Hare Law. The Minchmoor road then descends to the right but the Way remains up on another old drove road along the ridge. On the west approach to Brown Knowe it crosses a rampart and ditch known as Wallace's Trench, although it may be considerably older than the 13th century. Below can be seen the large ruined 15th century Douglas tower of Newark Castle, later taken over as a royal hunting seat, and also the SHYA's first hostel of Broadmeadows, opened in 1931. For access to the hostel, which lies a mile south of the Way, turn right at the crossing of paths at NT 421319. At Philiphaugh, in the valley below Broadmeadows Montrose's royalist army was surprised and defeated in 1645 by David Leslie's Covenant Army.

The Way continues to a trio of ten foot high drystone cairns called the Three Bethren on a rise elevated at 1500ft. Here met the lands of Selkirk Burgh, Yair and Philiphaugh, with one cairn in a corner of each estate. This is one of the places visited by the Common Riding, when in June riders process round the boundaries of the royal burgh of Selkirk partly in commemoration of thosed that died in the Battle of Flodden in 1513. The Way heads SSE before turning east again to enter forest. It crosses a forest track and turns left for a short distance on another and then descends as a faint path on the north side of a burn flowing down to meet the River Tweed at Yair. Here, by the kennels and stables, the Way turns right onto an estate road leading to where A707 crosses an 18th century bridge over the Tweed.

Minchmoor Bothy   *The Three Brethren*

Once over Yair Bridge continue round the left-hand bend of the main road a few yards and then take a track up the hill signed as a right of way past Fairnilee Farm. Cross over an estate road, glimpsing Fairnilee House of 1908 on the left, and just before Calfshaw turn left onto a steep track up to a gap between two small plantations. Then keep left of the wall until there is an old stile. At a junction of paths at NT 472343 keep right to pass through a small woodland and then turn left just before reaching a road to take a pretty path down the west side of a school. Turn right to find Barr Road on the NE side of Gale Hill unless you need the shops and other services of Galashiels, which is the centre of Scotland's tweed industry. The town has several mills, an old mercat cross, a statue of a Border Reiver and a mansion called Old Gala from which came a panel now at New Gala House dated 1583 with arms and initials of Andrew Pringle and Mariota Borthwick. An upper storey ceiling in the old building is dated 1635 with initials of Hugh Scott.

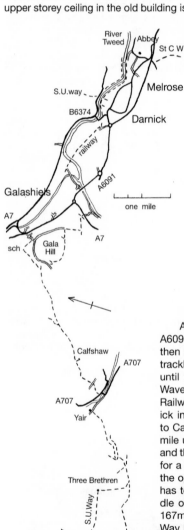

After a while Barr Road becomes a pleasant track with views across Galashiels, which straddles the valley of the Gala Water. There is an old tower called Appletreeleaves at NT494366 by a golf clubhouse above the other side of the valley, and, tucked out of sight further NW is a more impressive old ruined tower, that of Buckholm, a seat of the Pringles at NT 482378. When the track ends go straight on heading south with a wall on your left. Turn left and zig-zag down to cross over A7 and then down to turn left onto a lane on the NW bank of the Tweed. Beside it is the trackbed of a former railway branchline from Galeshiels to Selkirk opened in 1856 and closed in 1951.

On the opposite side of the Tweed is Sir Walter Scott's house of Abbotsford, open to the public in the summer months. He renamed what was a farm called Cartleyhole after purchasing it in 1811 and spent the next twenty years building the existing mansion in the Scots Baronial style, plus planting most of the trees now seen along the riverbank. Here almost all of his classic novels were written.

After going under a spectacular bridge carrying A6091 over the Tweed go over a roundabout and then after half a mile climb up to the right onto the trackbed of a railway, to cross the river. It was, in fact until 1969 the double-track mainline of the former Waverley route through the Borders. The North British Railway opened this section from Edinburgh to Hawick in 1849, although it was not completed through to Carlisle until 1862. The trackbed is followed for a mile until a path leaves on the left to cross a B-road and then follow the south bank of the River Tweed for a mile. The line of the Way heading north lies on the opposite bank after just a third of a mile but one has to go much further east, and closer to the middle of Melrose, to find a footbridge over the river, 167m from Portpatrick. Not far south of where the Way leaves the north bank opposite is the separate village of Darnick, with an inhabited T-plan tower dated 1569 with initials of Andrew Heiton and Katherine Fisher. Another building of c1600, a bastle (see page 42) rather than a tower, lies in ruins further south.

Abbotsford, Sir Walter Scott's house.

Melrose offers a range of shops and services, including a youth hostel and a tourist office. In 1136 David I founded here the first Cistercian abbey in Scotland, and it eventually became wealthy through sheep rearing. Because of its position it was vulnerable to English raids and invasions, and the present church dates from after a thorough destruction by Richard II of England in 1385. Part of a later high vault over the eastern part of the nave survives. The claustral buildings to the north and NW are mostly reduced to their foundations (see page 5). On the other side of a road is the semi-fortified house of the late 16th century commendator, or lay abbot, now a museum. Both this building and the abbey ruins are in the custody of Historic Scotland. The Scottish National Trust owns Priorwood Garden adjacent to the abbey, and there is a motor museum near the abbey mill. There is also a 17th century mercat cross. The Waverley Castle Hotel of 1869-71 (with a statue of Sir Walter Scott in the grounds) was one of the first concrete buildings in Scotland and lies on the edge of Skirmish Hill, where a battle took place in 1526.

The Commemdator's House at Melrose

Cross the Tweed on the chain suspension bridge of 1826 lying 300yards NW of the abbey and turn left along the north bank for over half a mile. Join B6374 and continue heading west along it for another 200yards before taking a path on the right, heading north up a hill. At a T-junction of roads take the road opposite and in 200yards turn right onto a track, keeping left at a fork after 400yards. This leads to a path over a shoulder of a hill rising 500ft above the river, and just east of Easter Housebyres. The path bends after a burn to run alongside a plantation and joins a probable former Roman road heading north. Cross over a road, and pass Bluecairn Farm (and Covenanters's Well) in a dip, and after almost two miles cross over a road onto another road. After two thirds of a mile turn left opposite Fordswell, passing left of a triangulation point in an old quarry at 900ft. The track becomes a path and does a slight left and right turn to cross a road. The path runs to the edge of the glen of Lauder Burn and descends to meet and eventually cross over it. Earthworks of a fort on Chester Hill to the right are now part of a golf course. On meeting a road in the village of Lauder turn right, then left past the church and right onto the A68 forming the main street 177m from Portpatrick. On an island in the middle of the road is the 18th century tolbooth, and there are shops, the 18th century Black Bull Hotel, and a house in which Sir John Cope spent the night after his defeat in 1714 by the Jacobites. The village is a conservation area and all its electricity cables were buried underground in 1975, which was European Architectural Heritage Year. The nearby bridge from which Archibald Douglas hanged James III 's despised favourites in 1482 no longer survives.

St Mary's church is a cruciform structure with a central tower with an octagonal top stage. It was built in 1673 by Sir William Bruce for William Maitland, then newly created Duke of Lauderdale by Charles II for his services as Scottish Secretary of State. His seat of Thirlestane lies just north of the village and here also lay the medieval church. Consisting of additionsdesigned by Bruce (plus some later work) to a main block with circular corner towers built by Sir John Maitland c1590, the castle lies on the site of a structure known as Lauder Fort. It is open to the public in the summer months, when there is a camp site in the grounds.

Thirlestane Castle, near Lauder

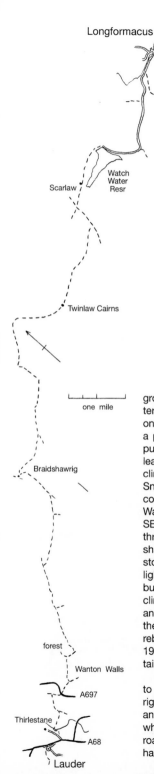

Longformacus

Scarlaw

Watch
Water
Resr

Twinlaw Cairns

one mile

Braidshawrig

forest

Wanton Walls

A697

Thirlestane

A68

Lauder

Lauder Church

At the SE end of Lauder turn left off A68 into the castle grounds and cross Leader Water on a footbridge. The path enters woods and climbs alongside the Earnscle Burn. Turn right onto a track up to A697 and cross over onto a farm track. Take a path on the left climbing from Wanton Walls past a water pumping station to Park Hall Plantation and turn right on a track leading out to the edge of the trees. Turn left over a stile and climb up near the woodland boundary. Descend to cross the Snawdon Burn and go over another ridge. Using a new bridge constructed by the armed forces as a training exercise, the Way then crosses Blyth Water and climbs up to pass down the SE side of a plantation. It then turns left onto a track passing through a gap between plantations and down towards Braidshawrig, fairly recently re-occupied. SE of the house a standing stone marks where the 12th Earl of Lauderdale was killed by lightning in 1884 whilst out shooting. Instead of crossing the burn over to the farm the Way swings right on a good track and climbs again onto Nun Rig. It eventually climbs onto a ridge and then a path follows the fence past Rutherford's Cairn to the barrel-shaped Twinlaw Cairns at 1500ft. Both cairns were rebuilt after destruction by Polish army training exercises in the 1940s. They have south-facing recesses, one of which contains a tin with a log-book like those found in the bothies.

The path improves as you descend heading east. Turn left to go north on a good track. Another track then leaves on the right to go through the yard of Scarlaw (site of an old tower) and round the north and east sides of Watch Water Reservoir, where there is a seasonal tearoom. From here are two miles of road-walking, mostly downhill, into Longformacus. This hamlet has a phonebox and b&bs, but no shop, pub or toilets

Abbey St Bathans Church

In Longformacus turn right onto a road and then left onto another road. Go a mile along it before taking a path climbing 250ft to pass round the south edge of Owl Wood. The path curves round and goes through a belt of trees and then descends through Lodge Wood to B6355. Turn left for a few yards to pass Whitchester Lodge, dated 1897, and then take a path on the right between plantations. After a while the path drops to the left to cross a burn and go through woodland above the south side of Whiteadder Water. Join a forest track and after two miles swing away from the river to reach a road opposite the church of Abbey St Bathans, 201m from Portpatrick. Here lay a Cistercian nunnery, and the east end of the church is medieval. It contains an effigy of a prioress.

Cockburnspath Church

The Way goes between the church and the former hostel opposite and crosses the river on a footbridge. It turns right to follow the river for 400yds before turning left to climb beside a tributary. It bends left and then goes between two newish plantations and climbs to pass Mr Cockburn of Whiteburn's rooster weathervane on a cairn and then cross over a road. After a while it turns left to reach another road.

Turn left along the road and then right on a track down to Blackburn Mill. Keep right at the junction of tracks beyond and climb to a crossroads of tracks and estate roads at Blackburn. Cross over and follow the road down for a mile and a half to A1. Do a slightly staggered cross over to gain the sections of old road now used as lay-bys. The road and railway were re-aligned in 1979 after a railway tunnel collapsed during an attempt to lower the tracks to take bigger freight containers, and the bodies of two workers still remain buried here. Use the bridge over the railway line and turn left to pass Penmanshiel, currently boarded up. About 400yards further on the Way turns back to the right and climbs through forestry. A clearing gives a view but you then descend to meet the track that you would have been on if you had kept straight on.

Turn right a short distance on A1107, away from the 120ft high viaduct of 1783 that takes it over Pease Dean, filled with sessile oaks, with ash and elm. The path then descends with flights of wooden steps to the burn. Cross the burn after the signboard offering shelter by an approach to a caravan site with a seasonal shop. Turn left to go uphill on the road to where there was once an inn with stables for the extra horses needed to pull coaches up from the Pease Dean gorge. Take the cliff-top path for a mile as it winds above Cove Harbour (see photo, page 11). A house down there has an access through a tunnel of the 1750s from the track to the pier. Folded rock strata is visible from the Way. Close to where the this track rises to the cliff-top turn inland and cross a road, then go under the railway and the A1. Turn left a short distance on the old A1 and then at the signboard go right to pass some toilets and appear in the square of the village of Cockburnspath, 212m from Portpatrick. The cross here commemorates the village being given as dowry to Henry VIII's sister Margaret Tudor when she married James IV of Scotland in 1503, and the ruined tower a mile SE of the village dates from that era. A track past the shop by the square leads past a three storey 16th century house known as Sparrow Castle (see page 38). The churchyard is reached directly off the square and contains a church which is partly 14th century. It has a thin 16th century circular bell-turret at the west end. Circular turrets or towers are rare in churches and it is a remarkable coincidence that old churches at the start and finish of the Southern Upland Way should both have circular belfries. At the east end the church has a 16th century slab-roofed burial aisle.

Cove Harbour

A1107

Dunglass

Pease Dene

forest

Cockburnspath   Tower

A1

Blackburn

Blackburn Mill

Whiteburn

Abbey St Bathans

Lodge   B6355

Owl Wood

one mile

Longformacus

ST CUTHBERT'S WAY

MELROSE - CRAILING

St Cuthbert's Way starts in Melrose where the saint established a monastery c650 and the marker posts of the trail bear an equal-armed cross symbol. On B6359 go south from the main square and the abbey and under the A6091 bypass. The Way then goes between houses on the left, dropping to cross a burn with a small wooded glen and then climbing 800ft from the height of the banks of the Tweed to a saddle at just over 1000ft between the main two volcanic peaks of the Eildon Hills. A big Iron-Age fort encircles the eastern peak, which is the lower of the two. Drop down to cross a path and enter woodland. Turn right onto a track, and go left onto a path which leads out of the woods and turns right, round the woodland edge and above a burn. Cross the burn after turning left and turn right down a track to the B6398 at Bowden. Go right a few yards then left on a lane. The Way turns left on a path but it is worth going a short distance round to the right to cross a burn and visit Bowden Church. The west and north walls are partly Norman, with one blocked original doorway. A north transept dated 1661 now contains the organ, and an east burial aisle of 1644 which is taller than the rest now forms the chancel.

Back at the corner the Way heads east to meet an estate road which crosses the Bowden Burn and rises above the south side. Keep heading along above the south edge of the burn and join a road for the last mile into Newtown St Boswells. Cross over B6398 and go under A68 to continue along the south bank of the burn until it meets the Tweed. The path then follows the south bank of the Tweed to where a pedestrian bridge allows access over to a folly Temple of the Muses on the left and then leads round to the right to the ruins of Dryburgh Abbey, now in the custody of Historic Scotland, where Sir Walter Scott and Field Marshal Earl Haig are buried. Founded c1150 for Promontratensian regular canons, the abbey has impressive remains of the domestic buildings and a fine chapter house, although only tall fragments remain of the church. Toilets are available outside of the abbey grounds, which lie 6m from Melrose Abbey. Distances quoted in this book include a mile added by the Bowden Church and Dryburgh Abbey detours.

Back at the bridge simply follow a path along the partly wooded south bank of the river. There is a short section at St Boswells without access so the Way cuts up to the B6404, and goes 400 yards left along it, passing a shop and pub, and then goes down a lane on the left back to the river-bank, which is followed until the tenth mile from Melrose and then inland a bit to climb up to Maxton Church. A mile and half can be saved by carrying on further down B6404 round a double bend in St Boswells to take a lane on the right for 200yards. Take a path to the left to get access back onto the river bank path.

Part of the ruined church of Dryburgh Abbey

Maxton Church

Maxton church is probably 16th century, see one of the doorways, but has been remodelled later. Go down a lane and turn right along a pavement beside A699, passing a water tap by houses before turning left onto a lane for a mile. Just before the lane reaches A68 turn left onto a path following the straight line of the Roman Road of Dere Street for three and a half miles. The path itself is far from straight and is pleasantly tree-lined. After a mile and a half there is an access into a field on the right where there is a memorial to a woman who valiantly fought alongside her lover against the English in the battle of Ancrum Moor in this locality in 1544. There is a campsite on A68 nearly opposite but no path cutting across to it.

Further along there is a tower called the Baron's Folly on the hill to the left. The path crosses a road and enters a plantation before bending right to cross over B6400. Shortly afterwards the Way turns left to skirt round the north side of Monteviot House, but a deviation to the right brings you to Harestanes Visitor Centre, with toilets. After crossing the drive to the house the Way crosses a field heading east and drops to join the bank of the River Teviot. A slight diversion off left goes to a boarded viewpoint. The Way heads west to cross a suspension bridge and then follows the south side of the river. Briefly join A6988 to cross Jed Water. Turn right onto a lane, then off left on a path climbing up on the line of the Roman Road again. After half a mile turn right onto Borders Abbeys Way to reach a campsite after a mile and a half. The services of the town of Jedburgh are another mile beyond it. Originally St Cuthbert's Way stayed on Dere Street for another mile and a half and then used four miles of roads to reach Cessford. It now turns off left just after the Jedburgh turn off and after a mile you can divert off left on a road to reach the village of Crailing beside A698.

Cessford Castle

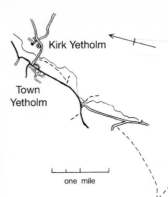

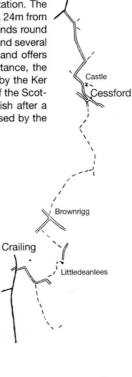

Turn right at the corner of a road where going left leads to Crailing. Clmb to a corner and take a track going left down to cross Oxnam Water. Follow the line of posts up around Littledeanlees and then climb up its access track to turn left on a path in a belt of trees at the top. Turn right then left on roads and go down the south side of Brownrigg to cross a burn in a belt of woodland. Climb again, bear right after going through a plantation, and turn left at a junction of paths at NT 716231 to go through another planatation. The path becomes a track bending right to drop into Cessford, 24m from Melrose. Cross the burn and turn left on a road which bends round to pass the castle ruin. There is free access into the field and several explanation boards. Although Cessford has few houses and offers no services to backpackers, it was once of great importance, the mid 15th century castle being the seat of a barony held by the Ker family, several generations of which served as wardens of the Scottish Middle March. The castle was wrecked by the English after a siege in 1523 and again in 1544, but was repaired and used by the Kers until c1650. They later became Dukes of Roxburgh.

The road past the castle leads to B6401, which is followed for a mile into Morebattle, 27m from Melrose, where there is a shop. Past the pub the main road goes left but the Way goes right onto a lane over the north end of Morebattle Hill. When the road bends left a drive on the right leads to Corbet (private) which has an old tower in the grounds (not visible from the Way). Turn right onto another road and follow it for 500yards until a footbridge takes you across Kale Water. From here there is a steep 700ft climb in under a mile to the 1080ft high summit of Grubbit Law. Cross over another path and stay on the top of a ridge to traverse Wideopen Hill and Crookedshaws Hill, with fine views of the Cheviots. Descend down to turn right onto a lane and then sharp left on a road heading north to meet B6401 towards Town Yetholm, where there is a shop and a pub. However the Way leaves the righthand side of the B-road after half a mile and uses a track which turns into a path beside Bowmont Water. Cross the river on a road leading up into Kirk Yetholm, although the Way reaches the village by means of a path following the river for 100yards and then curving right up to where the youth hostel is, 33m from Melrose. There is also a pub and several b&b's in the village, but no shop or toilets, although there is a water tap on the left as you climb out of the village.

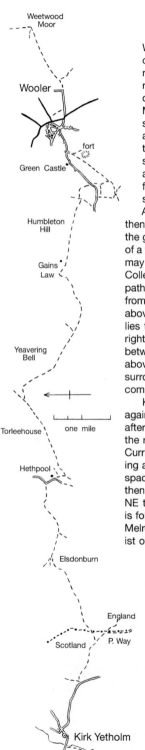

Kirk Yetholm marks the northern end of the Pennine Way and this route and St Cuthbert's Way both use the road climbing up to the east of the village. Both routes leave the road to cross Halter Burn after a mile and climb up below the ramparts of the Iron-Age fort of Green Humbleton. A quarter of a mile before the border with England is reached, 35m from Melrose, the Pennine Way heads SE whilst St Cuthbert's Way swings round left to head NE. It descends to cross a burn and then, at a stile, appears to enter a plantation, but in fact there is no way through so pass to the left round the northern side of the trees and head across a field to regain the path as marked on maps. A track then leads down to cross and follow the north side of Elsdon Burn. Notice the ancient, possibly prehistoric, cultivation terraces high above you.

At Hethpool, 38m from Melrose, turn right onto a reoad and then leave it on a path to the left at the next corner. Hidden in the gardens of the house are ivy-covered ruins two storeys high of a tower first mentioned in 1415, although the existing building may be later. It was held by the Collingwood family. Cross over College Burn and turn left to follow it before climbing up on a path through a plantation. The Way joins the drive coming down from Torleehouse, just before which are traces of a homestead above the right side of the path, whilst half a mile to the north lies the fort and settlement crowning West Hill. The Way turns right off the drive to climb up 600ft on the SW side of a valley between Easter Tor and Yeavering Bell. The latter, at about 1000ft above sea-level, bears remains of a ten foot thick drystone wall surrounding over 13 acres, a space large enough to contain a complete Iron-Age town, traces of which remain inside.

Keep heading SE at the junction of paths at NT 929281, and again onto a track at NT 935277. Leave on a path to the left after the track crosses a stream after 250yards, and head along the ridge towards Gains Law, 43m from Melrose. After passing Currick the path descends, increasing in steepness after crossing another path and turning to drop through woods to a picnic space by a road. Cross over and head up a valley heading south, then you can cut a corner off at NT 977266 turning left to head NE through a plantation. The path descends to a road, which is followed to the right down into the town of Wooler, 46m from Melrose. There are many shops, plus a youth hostel and tourist office. On a mound lie fallen fragments of a medieval tower.

Tumbled fragment of the castle at Wooler

St Cuthbert's Cave

From the middle of Wooler head down to cross over A697 onto B6348 for a short distance, then turn right into a path across the edge of playing fields out to a road heading up onto Westwood Moor. Turn left onto a path and keep climbing. Turn off left just before a plantation and drop steeply to cross over B6348 and take a lane crossing the River Till and passing Weetwood Hall. Ignore a road on the left and bend round to the right, following the lane for a mile to West Horton. Turn left at a road junction and then right onto a track, passing a wartime pill-box on the right in half a mile. The track descends to cross Hetton Burn, and bends left and right up to a road junction. Take the lane opposite heading east to Old Hazelrigg and turn left on what starts as a track but becomes a path. Ignore paths to the right and then left and then take a path on the right up to go left on a path just inside a plantation. After 350yards a path on the right leads up to a cavern known as St Cuthbert's Cave, 54 miles from Melrose.

Lindisfarne Castle

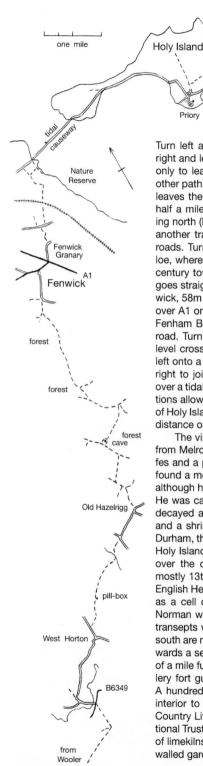

one mile

Holy Island

Castle

Priory

tidal causeway

Nature Reserve

Fenwick Granary

A1

Fenwick

forest

forest

forest cave

Old Hazelrigg

pill-box

West Horton

B6349

from Wooler

Either go past the path up to the cave and turn right when clear of the trees, or visit the cave and then clamber up a rough path to a gate to regain the Way and a view of the sea. Follow the path down over a stream and then up again to join a track with new North sea Trail signs. Turn left and go right after entering a plantation. Ignore right and left tracks but go left after the track bends right, only to leave it on a path on the right. This crosses another path, and then in 300yards crosses a track and then leaves the trees to skirt the plantation's east edge. After half a mile re-enter the plantation and keep right, heading north (luckily this is all fairly well signed). Turn right on another track leading down to a crossing of tracks and roads. Turning left for half a mile brings you to East Kyloe, where there remains the vaulted basement of a 15th century tower held by the Grey family. However the Way goes straight over onto the road, and drops down to Fenwick, 58m from Melrose. Turn right onto B6353 and cross over A1 onto a lane past Fenwick Granary. After crossing Fenham Burn go left onto a track which zigzags up to a road. Turn right, then left onto a path down to a railway level crossing. About 350yards beyond the crossing go left onto a track for 350yards and then take a path on the right to join a coastal path out to where a road crosses over a tidal causeway to Holy Island. When the tidal conditions allow follow this road for four miles out to the village of Holy Island, although at low tide you can do most of this distance on the sands (a nature reserve) if you prefer.

The village marks the end of St Cuthbert's Way, 64m from Melrose and is a tourist trap with several shops, cafes and a pub. Here St Aidan arrived from Iona in 635 to found a monastery of which St Cuthbert became bishop. although he died in a hermit's cell on Farne Island in 687. He was canonised after his body was found not to have decayed at all when exhumed ten years after his death, and a shrine to him was later set up in the cathedral at Durham, the location of the seat of the see since the 990s. Holy Island parish church is of Saxon origin (see the arch over the chancel arch) but the chancel and aisles are mostly 13th century. East of it lie the ruins (in custody of English Heritage) of a Benedictine priory built in the 1090s as a cell of the cathedral-priory at Durham. It has fine Norman work remaining in the aisled nave, crossing and transepts with east apses. The domestic buildings to the south are mostly later and more ruinous. A porch faces towards a semi-defensive outer court. On a rock two thirds of a mile futher east is the castle, a mid 16th century artillery fort guarding the anchorage (now a nature reserve). A hundred years ago Sir Edwin Lutyens remodelled the interior to make a retreat for Edward Hudson, owner of Country Life magazine. It is now administered by the National Trust. Just SE of the castle are an impressive group of limekilns of the 1860s whilst to the north of it is a small walled garden laid out in 1911 by Gertrude Jekyll.

THE JOHN MUIR WAY

COCKBURNSPATH - DUNBAR

In Cockburnspath take the road opposite the church entrance which goes past the school. A sign then points the way down a path along the edge of a wood. Cross a field with new gates to reach a path in woods on the south side of the Dunglass Burn. Cross the burn on a road bridge and take a road up to the left to visit the ruined mid 15th century church of Dunglass. The north transept is a burial place of the Humes and the south transept is a burial place of the Halls. Both transepts, the nave, and the chancel and the sacristy adjoining it retain original pointed vaults. Back at the junction by the bridge go NE on a signed path leading under the railway and A1. At a new sign turn left to visit the Iron Age fort of Castledykes with an impressive rampart on the landward side.

Back at the sign turn right down a path leading past the medieval bridge over the burn. A clearing in the vegetation just before where the path runs along the shingle beach offers a sheltered camping space. On reaching the Bilsdean Burn the path turns inland a short way before climbing though a tiny woodland belt to the top of low sandstone cliffs with several rock arches. At Thorntondean camping and caravan site there are public toilets. From here a diversion inland across the main road and railway can be made to reach a woodland path leaving a corner of the lane at Crowhill to reach the ruins of Innerwick Castle spectacularly placed on a sandstone crag above the gorge of the Thornton Burn. The castle belonged to the Hamiltons and had a tower and other buildings within a court defended on the north side by a rock-cut ditch. It was stormed by the English in 1547, when one man escaped by jumping down the cliff face, only to be shot by the assailants of Thornton Castle.

Sparrow Castle, Cockburnspath

Dunglass Church

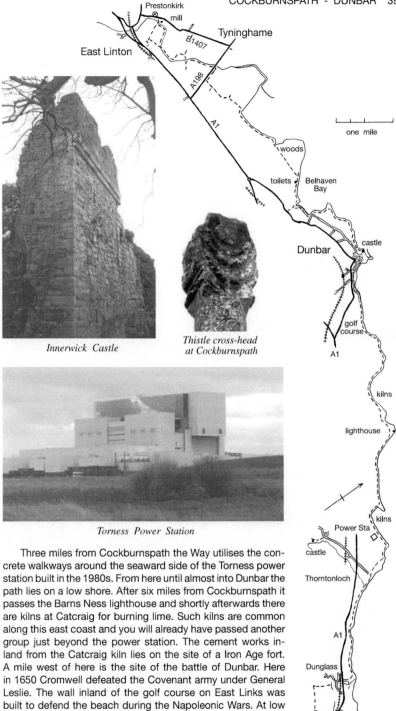

Innerwick Castle

Thistle cross-head at Cockburnspath

Torness Power Station

    Three miles from Cockburnspath the Way utilises the concrete walkways around the seaward side of the Torness power station built in the 1980s. From here until almost into Dunbar the path lies on a low shore. After six miles from Cockburnspath it passes the Barns Ness lighthouse and shortly afterwards there are kilns at Catcraig for burning lime. Such kilns are common along this east coast and you will already have passed another group just beyond the power station. The cement works inland from the Catcraig kiln lies on the site of a Iron Age fort. A mile west of here is the site of the battle of Dunbar. Here in 1650 Cromwell defeated the Covenant army under General Leslie. The wall inland of the golf course on East Links was built to defend the beach during the Napoleonic Wars. At low tide walking across nearly half a mile of beach is a more pleasant alternative to going along roads into the centre of Dunbar, which is ten miles from Cockburnspath.

Dunbar Castle from the east

Dunbar offers toilets, buses and trains to Edinburgh and Berwick and the south, and there are a fair range of shops, the main supermarkets being hidden away SW of the main street, close to the late medieval tower of the church of the Trinitarian friary, much altered by a conversion into a dovecot. The parish church near the station is of 1818 on the site of a fine 14th century collegiate church, from which has survived a monument to George Home, created Earl of Dunbar by James VI in 1605. A 17th century house with a polygonal stair-turret serves as a museum and has remains of the mercat cross in front of it. Almost opposite across the main street is the house in which the environmentalist and conservationist John Muir was born in 1838. Now a musum to his life and work, it is open free of charge seven days a week, although closed on Mondays and Tuesdays in winter. Perched on a rock are remains of the 13th century castle of the earls of Dunbar, scene of a remarkable defence by Black Agnes, Countess of Dunbar when attacked by the English in 1333. A wall across a bay connects the remains of the main court with a 16th century artillery bastion on a separate rock. The construction of the Victoria Harbour to the east begun in 1842 involved removing part of the castle to create the harbour entrance. At the other end is a battery of 1781 later occupied by an isolation hospital which lasted until 1927. Beyond is a smaller, older harbour with an east pier of the 1650s.

Although Dunbar forms a natural finish to the walk it is possible to continue for another seven pleasant and easy miles westwards to East Linton. The path rounds a series of small low sandstone headlands, passes a golf course, and then after two miles arrives at the John Muir Country Park. The circular building containing toilets has an external water-tap. The path then goes through trees to reach the south side of the estuary of the River Tyne, where there are display boards about the local wildlife. A track then leads to a new path along the edge of a field beside A198. An arch under the main road leads to a path on the south bank of the river. A footbridge by a ford then gives access to a track on the north bank of the river. After recrossing the river the Way turns right to follow its bank to another footbridge, but turn left for an alternative route the same distance which goes past the 16th century circular dovecot of Phantassie. Just beyond the footbridge lies Preston Mill, a 16th century watermill opened to the public by the National Trust for Scotland during the summer months.

Preston Mill

Between Preston Mill and Prestonkirk church the path passes a holy well, on the left after crossing a tributary of the river. The church has a main body and west tower of 1770 but the east end of a fine 13th century chancel has survived because it was the burial place of the Smeaton family. It has chamfered-cornered buttresses between lancet windows. From here follow B1407 westwards for a short distance to turn left on B1377 which forms the main street of East Linton, with a few shops. Buses for Edinburgh run along the main road at the bottom, which crosses the river on a 16th century bridge remodelled in 1763.

There is another section of John Muir Way linking Aberlady and Cockenzie by a shore path further west, but as yet this does not connect up with East Linton.

Prestonkirk Church

SOUTH LANARKSHIRE BASTLES TRAIL

Mostly built by tenant farmers in the period 1580-1620, bastle houses were a response to increased raiding across and along both sides of the Anglo-Scottish border in the late 16th century. (see Dryhope Tower on page 23). This general lawlessness only came to an end when James VI of Scotland succeeded the elderly Queen Elizabeth as James I of England and the border was forcibly pacified. Bastle houses were particularly numerous in Northumberland but more and more buildings of this type have been recognised in other counties both north and south of the Border over the last twenty five years. Bastles were plain buildings of modest dimenensions lacking wings, turrets, battlements or gunloops, i.e. defence was passive rather than offensive. Usually they had at ground level a roughly paved cattle byre with a central drain, and then above was a single living room with a fireplace and a few small windows fitted with iron bars. Some bastles had separate upper and lower entrances but the Lanarkshire bastles, most of which had vaulted byres and internal staircases, generally only had a single entrance in an end wall at ground level, the door being secured by a drawbar between two slots in the wall around waist-height.

Using Wanlockhead or Leadhills as a starting point a figure-of-eight shaped trail can be walked taking in part of the Southern Upland Way and visiting six bastles. Two of them are reduced to little more than foundations but walls up to ten feet high survive of the other four, although none of them preserve any worthwhile remains of an upper storey. Hidden away in in the hills at NT 016273 is another ruin of this type, Windgate House. Remains of others once existed at Thorril NS864309, beside M74, and Kirkhope, now under the waters of Daer Reservoir. Two others, Carnwath Mill NS 997454 and Nemphlar, NS 854447 retain their upper storeys, but are still in use and consequently have been altered over the years, whilst there are two more buildings, Howgate NS 920352 and St John's Kirk NS 983360, which are inhabited buildings incorporating older vaulted chambers from former bastles.

From the middle of Wanlockhead follow the Southern Upland Way for a mile and a third, and take a track climbing the slope on the the right just after the footbridge over Wanlock Water on the left. Cross the Glendorch Burn and make your way over Reecleugh Hill. There is not much actual path to follow so only attempt this in misty weather if your map and compass skills are good. Descend to the burn and follow its eastern side to Snar Farm. Gradually as you approach the farm there is more path to follow. Cross the burn to see the minimal remains of Snar Bastle at the south end of the farm buildings at NS 863201. Enough survives to show a wing was added to one end of the main block (see page 44) . It was excavated in the 1980s. The Douglas tenants here were primarily miners.

Glendorch Bastle, showing springing of former vault

Glenochar Bastle

Recross the burn and follow a clear track heading SE on the NE flank of Sim's Hill. Cross a burn after three quarters of a mile and then on the left is Glendorch Bastle NS 870188, one of the largest at 54ft long by 22ft wide. It belonged to the Foulis family, Edinburgh Goldsmiths, who had a lease of the nearby lead mines. Much of the south wall stands ten feet high with one small but well-made window, opening out of the largest of two lower rooms. On the other side of this wall are clear traces of a vault, and one jamb survives of the doorway further west. A shed, now derelict, was later built into the ruin.

The track becomes faint as it climbs almost up to 1500ft. After nearly a mile beyond Glendorch Bastle head off left through a gap in the ridge there and find a good track leading down into Leadhills, 9m from your starting point. As the name suggests, this was another mining community and it has a pub and a small shop. Take the B7040 heading east and after half a mile you can get onto the trackbed of an old mineral railway. It stays on the north side of the B-road for three miles and then crosses to the south side. When close to the electricity sub-station go round to the right to find Glengeith Bastle (NS947167). Only footings remain, on which are drystone walls supporting a modern shed (see page 44).

Cross over to A702 and walk southwards on it for two miles (it is quieter than one would expect). The next bastle, Glenochar, at NS 946139, 17m from the starting point, was excavated and conserved in the 1990s, and a trail has been made around its environs and outbuildings from a visitors' carpark on the main road. Traces of a stair adjoin the entrance and the lower room had a loop, vault and a central drain, indicating its use as a byre.

Remains of outbuildings at Glenochar

Shed on remains of Glengeith Bastle

Remains of wing added to Snar Bastle

Snar

Glendorch

Reecleugh
Hill

B797

S U W

cemetery

old railway

Leadhills

B7040

A702

Glengeith

Wanlockhead

one mile

B797

Glenochar

Lowther Hill

Allershaw
Lodge

Cold Moss

short cut through forest

Wintercleugh

Laight Hill

A702

forest

Smithwood

S U Way

SUW

forest

Daer
Reservoir

Entrance of Wintercleugh Bastle

Continue 300m further down the A702 and then turn left on the minor road. Take the track on the left after a mile which zig-zags up the hill between Allershaw Lodge and the burn. It climbs to 1200ft and then drops into a valley to end beside a fifth bastle, Wintercleugh at NS 980114. (not marked on Landranger map), 20m from the starting point. The remains have recently been conserved and show part of a stair next to the entrance.

Follow the winding burn for a mile down to the road and turn left towards the dam of the Daer Reservoir. Join the Southern Upland Way heading west by turning right at the cross-roads of roads and tracks in half a mile. Follow the Way as it leaves the road to turn right onto a forest track. Two hundred yards after the trees finish on the right-hand side look for the sixth and final bastle of the trail, Smithwood, at NS 959093, 22.5m from the starting point. again not marked on the Landranger map. Still undergoing conservation in 2005, the remains show evidence of vaulting, a central drain, a crosswall dividing the basement in two, and a doorway at the north end. The walls here are thinner than in the other bastles.

Follow the Southern Upland Way as it continues along the forestry track. At a junction turn left, then immediately take a path on the right down to a footbridge over Portrail Water and then alongside A702. In just under half a mile cross over A702 and the ditch marking a former Roman Road and climb 570ft in just over half a mile to the 1700ft high summit of Laght Hill. Drop 330ft into a saddle to the west and then climb up onto Comb Head and then Cold Moss and walk along the ridge forming the boundary between Lanarkshire and Dumfriesshire to the early warning system "golf ball" on the top of Lowther Hill. Follow the tarmac road down, although sections of path cut off the zig-zags, and then take the track descending into Wanlockhead to complete a circuit of just over 30 miles.

A possible alternative for a day walk is to park at the start of the Glenochar fermtoun trail and to go round in a circle of eleven miles via Wintercleugh, Daer, Smithwood, and use a possible short-cut return along the forest track leading north from NS 942098.

View NW from Lowther Hill

FURTHER READING

A History of Scotland, Rosalind Mitchison, 1970
Buildings of England Series: volume for Northumberland 2nd edition 1992
Buildings of Scotland series: volumes for Dumfries & Galloway and Lothian
Fortress Magazine, vol 5, 1990 (article about Lanarkshire bastle houses)
Royal Commission. on Ancient and Historical Monuments Inventories (various dates)
    for Wigtownshire, Kirkcudbright, Peebles, Selkirk,, Roxburgh and Berwickshire
Southern Upland Way: Offical Guide, two volumes by Ken Andrew, 1984
The Castles of South-West Scotland, Mike Salter, 2nd edition 2006
The Castles of Lothian and the Borders, Mike Salter, 1994
The Old Parish Churches of Scotland, Mike Salter, 1994
The Old Parish Churches of Northumberland, Mike Salter, 1997
The Steel Bonnets (The Story of the Anglo-Scottish Reivers), George McDonald Fraser

USEFUL WEBSITES AND OTHER INFORMATION

www.backpackersclub.co.uk - Club for those interested in backpacking in the UK.
www.campingandcaravanningclub.co.uk - Join to obtain details of extra camp sites.
www.dumgal.gov.uk/southernuplandway - Gives up to date information on any changes.
www.geocaching.com   - Finding caches using a Global Positioning System
www.ldwa.org.uk   - The Long Distance Walkers Association.
www.IndependentHostelGuide - Guide to independent hostels, new edition each year.
www.mountainbothies.org.uk - Club to join to find out details of over 100 bothies.
www.nationaltrail.co.uk   - Details of long-distance trails in UK.
www.southofscotlandcountrysidetrails.co.uk - Details of walking trails in Borders area.
www.syha.org.uk   - The Youth Hostels Association of Scotland.
www.traveline.org.uk   - Travel information throughout the UK
www.yha.org.uk   - The Youth Hostels Association of England and Wales.

National Rail Enquiries: 08457 48 49 50. For buses ring Traveline: 0870 608 2 608
Tourist Offices: open all year: Stranraer, Peebles, Jedburgh, Dunbar, Berwick
Tourist Offices: seasonal: Moffat, Galashiels, Melrose, Wooler
Youth Hostels: Kendoon 0870 001130   Broadmeadows 0870 0041106
    Melrose 0870 0041141   Kirk Yetholm 0870 0041132   Wooler 0870 7706100
    All Youth Hostels in Britain are open to non-members - at a small aadditional price.
Maps can be obtained through the Backpackers Club at a substantially reduced price.
The Backpackers Club provides members with info on farm and wild camping places.
Members of the Backpackers Club and the Long Distance Walkers Association obtain
    discounts on equipment from certain shops. Enquire for details.

Bowden Church